Cultures of Canada

Dance

Edited by
Heather C. Hudak

Weigl

Published by Weigl Educational Publishers Limited
6325 10 Street SE
Calgary, Alberta
T2H 2Z9

www.weigl.com

Library and Archives Canada Cataloguing in Publication data available upon request.
Fax 403-233-7769 for the attention of the Publishing Records department.

ISBN 978-1-55388-532-0 (hard cover)
ISBN 978-1-55388-537-5 (soft cover)

Printed in the United States of America
1 2 3 4 5 6 7 8 9 0 13 12 11 10 09

Editor: Heather C. Hudak
Design: Terry Paulhus

Every reasonable effort has been made to trace ownership and to obtain permission to reprint copyright material.
The publishers would be pleased to have any errors or omissions brought to their attention so that they may be
corrected in subsequent printings.

Weigl acknowledges Getty Images as one of its image suppliers for this title.
Alamy: pages 5 top left, 5 top right, 5 bottom right, 7 top left, 7 bottom left, 7 bottom right, 9 bottom left, 9 top right, 9 bottom right,
9 top left, 10, 11 top right, 11 bottom left, 12, 13 top right, 13 top left, 13 bottom left, 15 top left, 16, 17 bottom left, 19 top left, 19
bottom right, 19 bottom left, 19 top right, 20, 21 top left, 21 top right, 21 bottom right, 21 bottom left, 23 top left; Newscom: page 8.

All of the Internet URLs given in the book were valid at the time of publication. However, due to the dynamic nature of the Internet,
some addresses may have changed, or sites may have ceased to exist since publication. While the author and publisher regret any
inconvenience this may cause readers, no responsibility for any such changes can be accepted by either the author or the publisher.

We gratefully acknowledge the financial support of the Government of Canada through the Book Publishing Industry Development
Program (BPIDP) for our publishing activities.

Contents

Ukrainian Leaps and Spins

There are many Ukrainian dance groups in Canada. Ukrainian dances often use fast footwork.

The hopak is the best-known Ukrainian dance. This dance has fancy leaps and spins.

LEARN MORE
To learn about the hopak, visit www.wumag.kiev.ua/index2.php? param=pgs20064/144.

Ukrainian dancers often wear hats or headdresses? When do you wear a hat?

Red Boots

Hutzul Slippers

Headdress

Tunic

Chinese Folk and Classical Dances

There are two types of Chinese dance. Folk dances tell stories of love, war, farming, daily life, and celebrations. Dancers run and leap across the stage.

Classical dances are based on fairy tales and poetry. Dancers take small steps with their feet. They move their hands in special patterns.

LEARN MORE
To find out more about traditional Chinese dance visit www.houston cul.org/eng_culexg/c004.htm.

Fans are used in some Chinese dances. When have you used a fan? Did it look like the ones shown here?

Cheongsam

Headdress

Silk Fan

Shoes

Sikh Bhangra

Bhangra is a lively Sikh dance that celebrates the harvest. It is danced to dohls, or drums.

Bhangra is performed at Punjabi weddings, festivals, and other special events.

LEARN MORE
To learn more about bhangra and Punjabi culture, visit www.punjabonline.com/servlet/entertain.entertain?Action=Intro.

8

Sikh clothing is very colourful. What colours are the clothes you wear?

Ghagra

Kameez

Turban

Kurta

Iroquois Dance to the Beat

Some Iroquois dances are performed by men. Other dances are performed by women.

Dancers keep time to a beat. The beat is played on drums and rattles. Dancers move in a circle. They stomp or shuffle their feet.

LEARN MORE

Learn more about Iroquois dance at http://nativedrums.ca/index.php/ Music/Social_Dance?tp=a&bg=1&ln=e.

Traditionally, Aboriginal Peoples made clothes from items found in nature. What are your clothes made from?

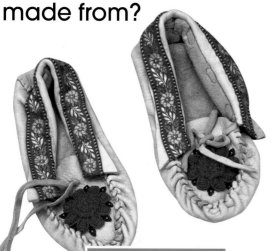

Moccasins

Fringed Pants

Feather Headdress

Beaded Shirt

Jewish Hora

The hora is a Jewish folk dance. It is often danced in a circle. People hold the hands of the people next to them. They place one foot behind the other as they step to the side.

Then, dancers move to the centre of the circle. They throw their joined hands in the air. They move back into the circle, and the dance starts again.

LEARN MORE
Learn more about Jewish dances at www.templesanjose.org JudaismInfo/song/dance.htm.

Some Jewish dancers wear an apron.
When might you wear an apron?

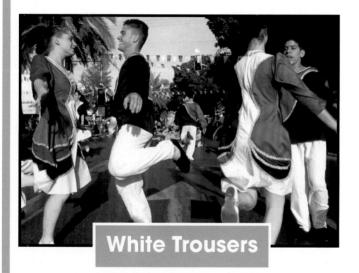

White Trousers

Apron

Peasant Blouse

Black Felt Hat

Spanish Flamenco

Flamenco is a Spanish dance. It is performed to the music of a guitar, singing, and hand clapping.

Dancers stomp their feet to make special sounds. They hold their arms above their head. Dancers turn their hands inward and outward as they move their arms.

LEARN MORE
Learn about flamenco and Spanish culture at www.enforex.com/culture/flamenco.html.

Spanish dance dresses have ruffles. What special features do your clothes have?

Short Jacket

High-waisted Pants

Ruffled Dress

Hair Comb

German Folk Dance

German dances often are performed by couples. Couples sometimes dance in large circles. There are also three-couple and four-couple dances.

Zwiefache is a German folk dance. The performer moves very little. The best dancers can dance in a very small space.

LEARN MORE
To learn about German folk dancing in North America, visit http://germandance.org.

German dancers often wear leather shorts with suspenders. How do suspenders work?

Lederhosen

Dirndl

Hat

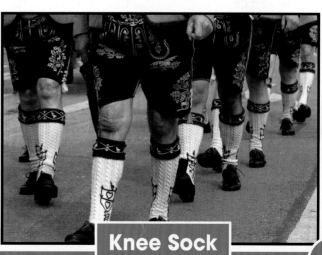

Knee Sock

French Cancan

The cancan is one of the best-known French dances. This dance is lively, with many high kicks. Today, it is danced only by women.

La Bastringue is a French-Canadian folk dance. Men and women perform this dance together.

LEARN MORE
Learn the words to the folk tune "La Bastringue" at www.terriau.org/music/bastring.htm.

White shirts are a common part of French dance outfits. What do the women wear on their shoulders and head?

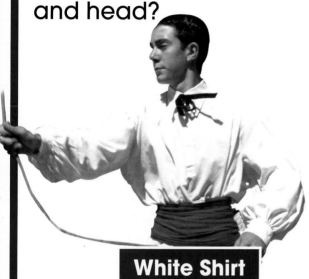

White Shirt

Black Pants

Gathered Skirt

Sash

Scottish Highland

Highland dancing is done mostly by the Scottish. Dancers perform ballet-like steps on the balls of their feet.

The Highland Fling takes great skill. The dancer must do difficult steps while staying in one place. Dancers do steps around swords in the Sword Dance.

LEARN MORE

Learn about the history of highland dance at www.maccullochdancers.ca/history.htm.

Scottish kilts are made from tartan.
What does the word "tartan" mean?

Ghillies

Kilt

Woollen socks

Vest

Filipino Balance and Bamboo

Each island in the Philippines has its own style of dance. Binasuan is one type of Filipino dance. Dancers put glasses of rice wine on their head and in each of their hands. They try to balance the glasses while they dance.

Tinikling is performed by two dancers. They hop between two bamboo poles. The poles are clapped together on the beat.

LEARN MORE
Learn about many dances from the Philippines at www.tagaloglang.com/Filipino-Culture/Philippine-Dances.

Some Filipino dance skirts are tube-shaped. What other types of skirts have this shape?

Bahag

Malong

Barong Tagalog

Apir

Glossary

apir: a fan

bahag: a cloth that hangs from the waist

barong tagalog: a lightweight, embroidered shirt

cheongsam: a straight, tight dress that has short sleeves, a high neck, and a slit skirt

dirndl: a full skirt that has a fitted waist

fringed: had a border of loose threads

ghagra: a flared skirt that reaches to the ankles

ghillies: shoes that have laces on the instep and do not have a tongue

Hutzul: a group of people from a certain part of Ukraine

kameez: a long shirt

kilt: a knee-length skirt that has a plaid pattern

kurta: a loose-fitting shirt that does not have a collar

lederhosen: leather shorts that have suspenders

malong: a tube-shaped skirt that has a colourful pattern

moccasins: shoes made from soft leather that do not have a heel

tunic: a long, loose, sleeveless shirt that reaches to the knees

turban: a head covering made from a long length of fabric

Index